CHILDREN'S PRAYERS

FROM AROUND THE WORLD

A LION BOOK

you wake me up
        Father
to a new day.
Thanks to you
I'm living.

Help me to live
        to day
as you wish.

From Sweden

Thank you Lord Jesus
for healing the lepers
and caring for the poor.
When you healed the lepers,
only one came back and thanked you
because all the rest were so excited
and ran to their friends.
Help us always to remember to thank you
for what you do for us.
Amen

From England

Lord, thank you for the rain
because it makes many plants live.
Lord, thank you for creating the earth
because on it there live many races.
I'd like so much that everybody prayed,
that everybody asked your forgiveness.
In the name of Christ I ask you.
Amen

From Brazil

I thank you for having freed us
from world wars,
and I ask that
you would bring peace to the world,
because it is so painful to know
that there are children in the world
that are losing their parents.
Please give light to the minds
and understanding of those
who are to blame for the wars
so that they know what they are doing.
I ask you because I know
you can do everything.
Amen

From Puerto Rico

Lord, we all belong to one another,
father, mother, my sisters and brothers and I.
We are one family.
We love one another.
Nevertheless we quarrel sometimes
when each of us wants our own way
and not what the others want.
Help me to find out
what the others would enjoy,
and when we have quarrelled,
help us to be kind again
to one another soon.
Amen

From Germany

Father God, some of us know
what it is to be afraid to talk to people
of a different religion.
We are afraid because of what our
parents will say or do to us.
We are afraid because of what our
neighbours will say or do to us.
Give us courage.
Teach children and grown-ups in this
and every land
to show love to people
no matter what colour they are
or by what name they are called.
Amen

From Northern Ireland

Hello, God.
How are you?
I am fine.
Dear God, stop the war.
I think wars are ugly.
Don't you think so too?
I don't write more now,
for then I would need a hundred papers.
So long, God.

From Sweden

God, thank you for the bread I ate today
Forgive all the evil I have done.
I hope mother likes my grades in school
as I have only one low gradexx.
Thank you.
Amen
From Brazil

I give thanks to God
because he has not left me alone in the world,
that I have a family that I love very much
and that they love me also.
I would like it if everyone in the world
had a family and that being together
could feel the warmth of love and care
the same as I feel.
Almighty God, I would like that there would be
no more hungry children in the world,
that people would stop thinking of killing
and would help the people that are so poor.
Amen

From Puerto Rico

Dear God,
thank you for your book the Bible
and all we can learn from it.
Thank you that you let your Son be crucified
for us even though we didn't ask.
Thank you for nice sunny days,
but please send some rain to the country
to fill the dams and to help the wheat
and other crops to grow.
Amen

From Australia

Lord Jesus, thank you
for dying for me.
You shed your blood for me:
thank you, Jesus Lord.
Forgive all my sins.
Let me see your face tonight.
O Jesus Lord, I love you.

From South Vietnam

Father God, some of us have learned to hate those
who go to a different school.
Some of us have thrown stones at children
just because they go to a different school
and a different church.
Forgive us, our Father,
for all the wrong things we have said and done.
Give us your Spirit
to help us to live and share with each other,
remembering you are the Father of us all.
Help people in every land to love their enemies
as well as their friends.
Amen

From Northern Ireland

Father is bad-tempered,
he is bad-tempered because of me.
I was rude to him.
Forgive me, Jesus!
It was wrong of me, but I didn't think.
I simply got into a rage.
Help him to forgive me,
and give me courage to ask his pardon!
You were never in a rage, Jesus,
even though you were also a boy once.
Do you understand me?

From Germany

Thank you for everybody on the earth
and thank you for the fish in the sea,
and dogs, cats and rabbits
to cuddle up with
when we're lonesome

(God, I hope you like my prayer)

From the United States

Gentle Jesus, be with us today.
I ask you, give us all our daily needs.
Gentle Jesus, I ask you to be with all those
in hospitals.
Give them strength to pray to you.
Be with our parents at home.
Jesus, be with us as we talk to you every day
and listen to you.
Be with those who are sad.
Let them know that you are their Father
so they cannot feel alone.
Be with us now and for ever.
Amen

From Namibia

Mother is bad-tempered, Jesus,
she can't manage her work.
She has too much to do,
and I don't feel like helping her.
Make me want to help her!
Don't let me wait till she asks me.
Show me that it can be fun to help,
so that mother won't be so tired any more.
Amen

From Germany

Jesus, Lord, it hurt you so much to be crucified.
Thank you, Lord, for being wounded for me.
Truly the devil tempts me every day;
Jesus, Lord, I don't want to see him:
I want to see you in my dreams.

From South Vietnam

Our dear Lord,
thank you for bringing me
to this children's home.
Before I didn't know you,
and I always quarrelled and took away things
which were not mine.
I was lazy.
Now I don't do it any more
because you told me in your book, the Bible.
I am now happy.
Thank you Lord.

From the Philippines

Dear God,
please help me not to get nightmares,
and to get to sleep
so I can get up for school next day.
Help me not to disobey my mummy and daddy
when they tell me to do something,
and help me not to answer back.
Please help me to be kind to my friends
and to do my best at school
so that I can please Jesus, your Son.

From England

My good Lord, I want that you
take care of the poor,
help me in school
and give happiness to everybody.
I would like men to stop their madnesses,
to stop polluting the waters and the fresh air
and to stop burning the trees.
If you, Lord, do all this I'll be very thankful.
It is only this that I want, my good Lord.
Amen

From Brazil

God, what kind of world is this
that the adult people
are going to leave for us children?
There is fighting everywhere
and they tell us we live in a time of peace.
You are the only one who can help us.
Lord, give us a new world
in which we can be happy,
in which we can have friends
and work together for a good future.
A world in which there will not be
any cruel people
who seek to destroy us and our world
in so many ways.
Amen

From Liberia

For all children
who don't have a bed to sleep in
and don't get as much food
and help and care as we,
for all children
who don't have their own quiet corner
or toys to play with,
for children
who must go away from their home,
from father and mother —

I'm praying: God protect them!
Send someone to their rescue
and let them get a home.

From Sweden

God, one of my teachers told us in class
that in some countries white people
don't like black people.
But the Bible says that you made everybody in the world.
So please try and make people stop hating one another
and rather love one another instead.
I believe that will stop all the wars
and bring peace.

From Liberia

We thank you, our God, because
you do so many good things for us.
We have no nice words to thank you
but you listen to us.
Lord, you protect us day and night,
we have no power to help ourselves.
Our Father, we leave ourselves in your hand.
Amen

From Namibia

Father God, we have a beautiful country
with green fields and hills and valleys and lakes.
Our fields grow good crops.
We always have enough to eat.
We have good schools and hospitals.
We have many churches and leaders and teachers.
Forgive us for taking these gifts for granted.
Forgive us for wasting things.
Forgive us for not sharing with others in need.
Help people in rich countries like ours
to care about poorer countries.
Amen

From Northern Ireland

Thank you Lord for food,
And for this lovely day.
Help us in coming weeks
And those who are astray
AMen

From Australia

My God, I thank you for my food.
It is you that allows the rice,
the beans, the wheat, the fruit,
the animals and the vegetables to grow.
I thank you for the food
that is on the table.
Thank you very much, Lord.
Amen

From Brazil

God has given me a voice and a tongue.
I can shout, whisper, sing.
God made the mouth to speak good words.

Teach me, God, to thank and praise,
and with words and deeds
show that I am your child
and want to belong to the kingdom of heaven.

From Sweden

Jesus, you're alive!
Not as you were alive in Galilee with your friends.
Then only the people who met you could talk to you —
but now, everybody can.

I'm talking to you and you're with me;
friends of yours all over the world
are talking to you now, this very minute,
and you're with them.

That's what I like about you —
alive for everyone.

From Holland

Dear God:
Thank you for the flowers.
                          Amen

O God:
Thank you for our
families, and for
  Our homes, and pets,
and food and TV.
                    Amen

O God:
Thank you for your love. Amen

Dear God:
We love you. Thank you for
Jesus and for our church.

Help our pastor and
  teachers . Amen

From the United States

Dear God,
please help all the
neglected people in the world
who can't just go into the kitchen
and get a sandwich.

From Australia

Lord, I pray for my poor father.
He works so hard and tries so hard to help
my mother and us the children.
But his salary is so small he cannot do all
the things he wants to do for us.
Help us to be good children who love him,
and who will encourage him
to keep his trust in you.
Some day, we believe,
everything will be all right.

From Liberia

Dear Lord,
in your word you teach us to love one another.
We ask you, dear Jesus,
prevent war and bloodshed,
prevent us and all the others
from hunger and sickness.
Let people stop killing each other.
Forgive us our sins in your name alone.
Amen

From Namibia

Dear God,
please be with us as
we play at school,
so that noone will get hurt,
and please help there to
be no arguments
during the game.
Amen

From Australia

Dear Jesus,
I'm very happy to be here in this home
although I have no father, mother,
sister and brother.
Now I have because I found you.
Thank you for sending people to help us
to buy our food, clothes and things we need.
I love you, Jesus.

From the Philippines

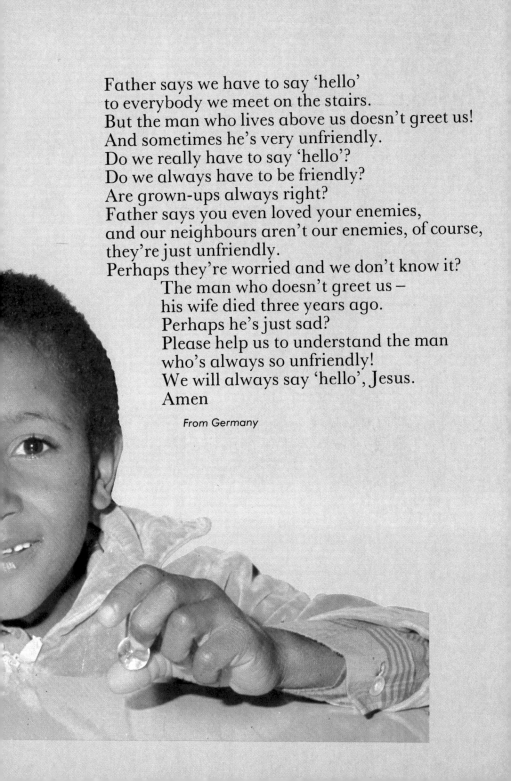

Father says we have to say 'hello'
to everybody we meet on the stairs.
But the man who lives above us doesn't greet us!
And sometimes he's very unfriendly.
Do we really have to say 'hello'?
Do we always have to be friendly?
Are grown-ups always right?
Father says you even loved your enemies,
and our neighbours aren't our enemies, of course,
they're just unfriendly.
Perhaps they're worried and we don't know it?
      The man who doesn't greet us –
      his wife died three years ago.
      Perhaps he's just sad?
      Please help us to understand the man
      who's always so unfriendly!
      We will always say 'hello', Jesus.
      Amen

From Germany

Lord, I ask you
to help those
who lost
their houses,
their crops
and everything that
belonged to them.
Help me also
to pass
in the school,
not only me,
but also my friends.
I thank you for everything
that you have given us.

From Brazil

Almighty God,
I pray for those who are in danger
and, O God, give to those who don't have anything.
I pray for my country
that you will be merciful to it.
Almighty God,
I pray for my teachers.
I pray for the hospitals
and I pray for the farmers
who give us rice to eat.
I pray for those who are on the seas.
I pray for myself,
to forgive me the sins
that I have committed for the day.
Through Jesus' name,
Amen

From Sierra Leone

God, thank you for helping
that I can be in a good school like this.
This school even has religion classes
which is what I most wanted.
Please make that I can always have
good schools like this
and that my mother will be able to pay
for our food, water, house and school.
Amen

From Brazil

Dear Lord, I try to study hard
but when tests are given I don't make good grades.
Why?
I know my teacher is sometimes cruel.
He takes points out for every little mistake.
Sometimes I think he does that for my own good
but sometimes I am not so sure.
I pray you to help me understand my problem
so that I can pass.
I don't want my pa and ma to be angry with me
every time I fail maths.
So help me to study and know maths.
Amen

From Liberia

Thank you God for happy days,
Christmas, birthdays,
and time for playing with toys.
Thank you God for holidays,
walking on the pier,
playing on the soft warm sand,
and swimming in the bouncing sea.
I like to watch the waves tossing around,
as they remind me of your love all round us.

From England

The alarm rang and I have to get up, Jesus,
but I'm not really looking forward to this day.
Who knows what's going to happen?
Please make me cheerful, Jesus,
and make this a nice day!
Amen

From Germany

God, I am sick
Heal my right eye
I cannot see well and I need
to be operated.
I am afraid but I know
you are near me.
Thank you God.

From the Philippines

My Jesus,
I think about so many mistakes and sins
I have done getting away from you.
Forgive me!
I want to improve my life,
showing my love and happiness
for having you close to me.
Amen

From Brazil

Dear God.
I just feel good knowing that
you are everywhere.
That's all
From Sweden

Copyright © 1981 Lion Publishing

Published by
Lion Publishing
Icknield Way, Tring, Herts, England
ISBN 0 85648 353 2
Albatross Books
PO Box 320, Sutherland, NSW 2232, Australia
ISBN 0 86760 288 0

First edition 1981

Acknowledgements
We would like to thank the Lutheran World
Federation, Geneva, Switzerland, for giving us
permission to use the following prayers, taken
from their publication *Children in conversation
with God:* pages 6, 9, 10, 12, 13, 14 (above), 17,
18, 19, 20 (above), 24, 25, 26 (above and middle),
29, 30 (above), 31, 33, 35, 36, 38, 39, 42 (above
and below), 44.
Other prayers are reproduced by kind permission
of: Community of the Glorious Ascension, page 30
(below); Dove Communications, Australia, page
32, from *You can hear him listening;* Stuart
Harverson, pages 15, 20 (middle), from *Doctor in
the Orient,* Hodder and Stoughton Ltd.
Thank you also to the children from Ladymede
School, Little Kimble, Buckinghamshire, who
wrote out the prayers on pages 6, 13, 15, 18, 28,
31, 32, 34, 42 and 44.

Photographs reproduced by kind permission of the
following photographers and organizations:
Compassion International Inc., USA, page 8;
Lion Publishing: David Alexander, pages 18 and
40; Tony Cantale, pages 40 and 41, Jon Willcocks,
pages 7, 16 and 17, 30; Jean-Luc Ray, pages 5,
11, 19, 33, 37 (above); Nick Rose, page 17;
Nicholas Spurling, pages 44 and 45; all remaining
photographs from TEAR Fund, 11 Station Road,
Teddington, Middlesex, a Christian agency
engaged in relief and development projects
throughout the Third World.

Printed in Spain by Artes Graficas, Toledo
D.L. TO: 673 - 1981